Contents

Projected Costs of
U.S. Nuclear Forces, 2014 to 2023

Summary

In its most recent review of U.S. nuclear policy, the Administration resolved to maintain all three types of systems that can deliver nuclear weapons over long ranges—submarines that launch ballistic missiles (SSBNs), land-based intercontinental ballistic missiles (ICBMs), and long-range bombers—known collectively as the strategic nuclear triad. The Administration also resolved to preserve the ability to deploy U.S. tactical nuclear weapons carried by fighter aircraft overseas in support of allies. Nearly all of those delivery systems and the nuclear weapons they carry are nearing the end of their planned operational lives and will need to be modernized or replaced by new systems over the next two decades. In addition, the Administration's review called for more investment to restore and modernize the national laboratories and the complex of supporting facilities that maintain the nation's stockpile of nuclear weapons. The costs of those modernization activities will add significantly to the overall cost of the nation's nuclear forces, which also includes the cost of operating and maintaining the current forces.

As directed by the Congress in the National Defense Authorization Act for Fiscal Year 2013 (Public Law 112-239), the Congressional Budget Office (CBO) has estimated the costs over the next 10 years of the Administration's plans for operating, maintaining, and modernizing nuclear weapons and the military systems capable of delivering those weapons. CBO's estimates should not be used directly to calculate the savings that might be realized if those forces were reduced: Because the nuclear enterprise has large fixed costs for infrastructure and other factors, a partial reduction in the size of any segment of those forces would be likely to result in

savings that were proportionally smaller than the relative reduction in force.

How Much Funding Did the Administration Request for Nuclear Forces in 2014?

The budgets requested by the Department of Defense (DoD) and the Department of Energy (DOE) for fiscal year 2014 include $23.1 billion for nuclear delivery systems and weapons, CBO estimates—$9.7 billion for DoD's strategic and tactical nuclear delivery systems; $8.3 billion for DOE's nuclear weapons activities, the laboratories that support those activities, and nuclear reactors for ballistic missile submarines; and $5.1 billion for the command, control, communications, and early-warning systems that are necessary to operate U.S. nuclear forces safely and effectively (see Table 1).

In addition to the costs directly attributable to fielding nuclear forces, the costs of several related activities are included in some published estimates of the cost of nuclear weapons. Examples include the costs of addressing the nuclear legacy of the Cold War, including dismantling retired nuclear weapons and cleaning up the environment around contaminated historical nuclear facilities; the costs of reducing the threat from nuclear weapons fielded by other countries, including efforts to halt proliferation, comply with arms control treaties, and verify that other countries comply with their treaty obligations; and the costs of developing and maintaining active defenses against nuclear weapons from other countries, primarily defenses against ballistic missiles. CBO estimates that DoD's and DOE's budgets for 2014 include $20.8 billion for such other nuclear-related activities, comprising $7.0 billion for nuclear legacy costs, $3.2 billion for threat reduction and arms control, and $10.6 billion for defenses.

Table 1.

Costs of U.S. Nuclear Forces

(Billions of dollars)

Category	2014	Total, 2014 to 2023
Budgeted Amounts for Nuclear Forces[a]		
Nuclear delivery systems	9.7	136
Nuclear weapons, supporting laboratories, and naval reactors[b]	8.3	105
Subtotal	18.0	241
Command, control, communications, and early-warning systems	5.1	56
Total Budgeted Amounts for Nuclear Forces	**23.1**	**296**
Additional Costs Based on Historical Cost Growth	n.a.	59
Total Estimated Cost of Nuclear Forces	**23.1**	**355**
Memorandum:		
Budgeted Costs of Other Nuclear-Related Activities[c]	20.8	215

Source: Congressional Budget Office based on information from the Department of Defense and the Department of Energy.

Note: n.a. = not applicable.

a.   This category is based on CBO's analysis of the budget proposals of the Department of Defense and Department of Energy and accompanying documents, as well as CBO's projection of those budget figures under the assumption that programs will proceed as described in budget documentation. The category also includes several programs for which plans are still being formulated; in those cases, CBO based its estimate on historical costs of analogous programs. The budgeted amounts should not be considered independent estimates by CBO of the costs of U.S. nuclear forces.

b.   This category includes $400 million in 2014 and $4 billion over the 2014–2023 period for funding of naval reactors for strategic ballistic missile submarines only.

c.   This category includes legacy costs of nuclear weapons and infrastructure, costs for threat reduction and arms control, and costs for missile defense and other defenses (see Box 1 on page 6).

What Will the Administration's Plans for Nuclear Forces Cost Over the Next Decade?

Between 2014 and 2023, the costs of the Administration's plans for nuclear forces will total $355 billion, in CBO's estimation. Of that total, $296 billion represents CBO's projection of the amounts budgeted for strategic and tactical nuclear delivery systems ($136 billion over 10 years); for nuclear weapons, DOE's nuclear weapons enterprise, and SSBN nuclear reactors ($105 billion over 10 years); and for nuclear command, control, communications, and early-warning systems ($56 billion over 10 years). The remaining $59 billion of the total represents CBO's estimate of the additional costs that will ensue over the coming decade, beyond the budgeted amounts, if the nuclear programs experience cost growth at the same average rate that similar programs have experienced in the past.

In addition to operating and maintaining current systems, DoD and DOE plan to modernize or replace many

weapons and delivery systems over the next few decades. Planned nuclear modernization programs include new SSBNs, long-range bombers, ICBMs, and cruise missiles, as well as major life-extending refurbishments of current ICBMs, submarine-launched ballistic missiles, and nearly all nuclear warheads. Of the $241 billion budgeted for nuclear delivery systems and weapons over the next 10 years (combining the $136 billion and $105 billion figures in the preceding paragraph), CBO estimates that $152 billion would be spent to field and maintain the current generation of systems and $89 billion would be spent to modernize or replace those systems. Because most of those modernization efforts are just beginning, annual costs for nuclear forces are expected to increase. From 2021 to 2023, nuclear costs would average about $29 billion annually, roughly 60 percent higher than the $18 billion requested for 2014. Annual costs are likely to continue to grow after 2023 as production begins on replacement systems.

CBO formulated its estimates using a three-step approach: identify all budget line items relevant to nuclear forces; extrapolate from budget documentation, as necessary, to estimate budgets over the 10-year period (most of DoD's programs have five-year estimates); and estimate cost growth beyond budgeted amounts on the basis of historical growth in similar programs. CBO estimated cost growth for various types of activities on the basis of historical average growth for similar activities because predicting cost growth for individual programs is particularly complicated. CBO used only the unclassified portion of DoD's budget to formulate its estimates.[1]

The costs of other nuclear-related activities will total $215 billion from 2014 to 2023, CBO estimates, with $74 billion in legacy nuclear costs, $34 billion for threat reduction and arms control, and $107 billion for defenses.

What Are the Most Significant Sources of Uncertainty in CBO's Estimates?

There are two primary aspects of uncertainty in CBO's estimates of the costs of nuclear forces: The actual cost of executing current plans could be higher or lower than CBO has estimated, and the plans on which the estimates are based could change.

In terms of estimating the cost of current plans, the largest source of uncertainty is cost growth. Although CBO based its projections of cost growth on historical experience, the amount of growth that will actually occur could be higher or lower than in the past. Another source of uncertainty is the allocation of costs for systems that have both nuclear and nonnuclear missions. CBO estimated the fraction of those systems' total costs that pertained to the nuclear mission; different estimates of those values would yield somewhat different cost estimates for nuclear forces.

Uncertainty also arises from the possibility that plans will change, which could occur for several reasons, including budgetary pressures, technical difficulties in the development of new systems, or changes in military strategy. One significant source of uncertainty of this type is that DoD

and DOE are still formulating the plans for several new systems—specifically, the new long-range bomber, the new cruise missile, the future ICBM, and a new concept for modernizing warheads that would make them compatible with both ICBMs and submarine-launched ballistic missiles. Future plans for nuclear forces might also change if the budgets of DoD and DOE are reduced between 2014 and 2021 to comply with the funding caps enacted in the Budget Control Act of 2011 (as modified by subsequent legislation). Those funding caps are about 14 percent below CBO's projection of the costs of the Administration's defense plans, on average, for those years; a proportional cut in the cost of nuclear activities would total $39 billion between 2014 and 2021.[2]

Costs of Nuclear Forces

Although the U.S. nuclear arsenal is substantially smaller today than at the height of the Cold War, U.S. nuclear weapons still "play an essential role in deterring potential adversaries and reassuring allies and partners around the world," according to the Administration's most recent *Nuclear Posture Review Report*, published in April 2010. The ability of the United States to field credible and reliable nuclear forces involves many disparate efforts, including operating and maintaining the missiles, aircraft, and submarines that would deliver the weapons; performing scientific research, maintenance, and testing to ensure the nuclear weapons remain safe and reliable; and fielding communications satellites that are robust enough to operate in the harsh environment that would result from a nuclear exchange.

From its beginning in the Manhattan Project, the U.S. nuclear weapons enterprise has involved the combined efforts of military and civilian organizations. The names of those organizations have changed over the years, but

---

1. Most nuclear programs have some classified aspects, but their budgets are generally unclassified. Although some programs, primarily related to intelligence, have classified budgets that may include costs related to nuclear weapons, the vast majority of nuclear costs are included in the unclassified budget.

2. The funding caps are about 10 percent below CBO's projection of the budgeted amounts for defense plans as of November 2013 (leaving aside CBO's estimate of cost growth beyond the budgeted amounts). Therefore, a proportional cut in the cost of nuclear activities would total $23 billion between 2014 and 2021. For CBO's projection of the overall defense budget, see Congressional Budget Office, *Long-Term Implications of the 2014 Future Years Defense Program* (November 2013), www.cbo.gov/publication/44683. The Bipartisan Budget Act of 2013, which had just been passed by the Congress when this report was released, would have only a small effect on the cumulative limit on defense funding for 2014 through 2021. Therefore, updating these calculations to incorporate the effect of that act would have little impact on the conclusions presented here.

the basic partnership established in the Atomic Energy Act of 1946, in which a civilian agency has responsibility for nuclear weapons and the military has responsibility for the systems and personnel that would deliver those weapons, persists today. The Department of Energy is the civilian agency responsible for nuclear weapons; the Department of Defense is responsible for the delivery systems.

In this report, the Congressional Budget Office provides detailed estimates of the costs of activities at those two departments in support of nuclear forces over the next 10 years. For 2014, DoD requested $14.9 billion for nuclear forces, including strategic and tactical delivery systems and command, control, communications, and early-warning systems (see Table 2). DOE requested $8.3 billion to support work related to nuclear weapons (for specific types of warheads and for general support of the nuclear weapons stockpile) and to design, build, and maintain nuclear reactors on ballistic missile submarines. Between 2014 and 2023, DoD's plans would cost $191 billion and DOE's plans would cost $105 billion, for a combined 10-year cost of $296 billion for nuclear forces, by CBO's projection of the departments' budget figures. In addition, CBO estimates that if costs to modernize weapons and delivery systems and to construct new nuclear facilities continued to grow as they have historically, then costs would be $59 billion higher ($30 billion higher for DoD and $29 billion higher for DOE), which would boost the total 10-year cost for nuclear forces to $355 billion.

Throughout this report, CBO's program-by-program estimates reflect the assumption that DoD's and DOE's plans would be executed successfully and on budget—that is, the program-by-program estimates do not incorporate any cost growth beyond that assumed by DoD or DOE. The additional costs that would ensue if the costs of nuclear modernization programs and facilities continued to grow as they have in the past are presented only in some of the budgetary totals.

To analyze the costs of operating, maintaining, and modernizing U.S. nuclear forces, CBO examined the parts of DoD's and DOE's budgets that are associated with the following functions:

- Strategic nuclear forces, which deliver nuclear weapons over long distances. Those forces consist of three "legs" and are thus known as the triad: submarines that launch ballistic missiles (including submarines and associated ballistic missiles, nuclear reactors, and nuclear warheads); intercontinental ballistic missiles (including missiles and associated nuclear warheads); and long-range bombers (including aircraft and associated nuclear weapons). All three legs depend on funding from both DoD and DOE.

- Tactical (or short-range) nuclear forces (including aircraft purchased and operated by DoD and associated nuclear weapons maintained by DOE).

- Nuclear command, control, communications, and early-warning systems operated by DoD.

- All activities at DOE's nuclear weapons laboratories that are not attributed directly to a specific warhead type but are related to maintaining current and future stockpiles of weapons.

Of the $296 billion that CBO projects for the next decade based on analysis of the departments' budgets, $156 billion would be for strategic nuclear forces ($132 billion for delivery systems and $25 billion for warheads and nuclear reactors); $7 billion would be for tactical nuclear forces ($4 billion for delivery systems and $3 billion for warheads); $56 billion would be for command, control, communications, and early-warning systems; and $77 billion would be for DOE's nuclear weapons enterprise (excluding costs associated with sustainment and modernization activities unique to specific warhead types).

For each of those functions, CBO analyzed the relevant budgets by appropriation title. For DoD, the relevant titles are military personnel; operation and maintenance; procurement; and research, development, test, and evaluation (RDT&E).[3] For DOE, the relevant titles are part of the National Nuclear Security Administration's (NNSA's)

---

3. Over the next five years, DoD's plans include about $300 million for military construction related to nuclear weapons forces. Because of the difficulty in predicting future construction needs, CBO has not projected military construction budgets beyond 2018.

Table 2.

Costs of U.S. Nuclear Forces, by Department and Function

(Billions of dollars)

Category	2014			Total, 2014 to 2023		
	DoD	DOE	Total	DoD	DOE	Total
Budgeted Amounts for Nuclear Forces[a]						
Nuclear delivery systems and weapons						
Strategic systems						
Ballistic missile submarines	5.1	0.9	6.0	71	11	82
Intercontinental ballistic missiles	1.4	0.2	1.6	20	4	24
Bombers	1.7	0.4	2.2	29	10	40
Other nuclear activities[b]	1.0	n.a.	1.0	11	n.a.	11
Subtotal	9.3	1.5	10.8	132	25	156
Tactical delivery systems and weapons	0.4	0.3	0.7	4	3	7
Nuclear weapons laboratories and supporting activities						
Stockpile services	n.a.	0.9	0.9	n.a.	12	12
Facilities and infrastructure	n.a.	2.5	2.5	n.a.	30	30
Other stewardship and support activities[c]	n.a.	3.1	3.1	n.a.	35	35
Subtotal	n.a.	6.5	6.5	n.a.	77	77
Total, Nuclear Delivery Systems and Weapons	**9.7**	**8.3**	**18.0**	**136**	**105**	**241**
Command, control, communications, and early-warning systems						
Command and control	1.3	n.a.	1.3	13	n.a.	13
Communications	2.0	n.a.	2.0	23	n.a.	23
Early warning	1.9	n.a.	1.9	20	n.a.	20
Subtotal	5.1	n.a.	5.1	56	n.a.	56
Total Budgeted Amounts for Nuclear Forces	**14.9**	**8.3**	**23.1**	**191**	**105**	**296**
Additional Costs Based on Historical Cost Growth	n.a.	n.a.	n.a.	30	29	59
Total Estimated Cost of Nuclear Forces	**14.9**	**8.3**	**23.1**	**221**	**134**	**355**

Source: Congressional Budget Office based on information from the Department of Defense and the Department of Energy.

Note: DoD = Department of Defense; DOE = Department of Energy; n.a. = not applicable.

a.   This category is based on CBO's analysis of the budget proposals of the Department of Defense and Department of Energy and accompanying documents, as well as CBO's projection of those budget figures under the assumption that programs will proceed as described in budget documentation. The category also includes several programs for which plans are still being formulated; in those cases, CBO based its estimate on historical costs of analogous programs. The budgeted amounts should not be considered independent estimates by CBO of the costs of U.S. nuclear forces.

b.   This category includes nuclear-related research and operations support activities by DoD that CBO was not able to associate with a specific type of delivery system or weapon.

c.   Activities include scientific research and high-performance computing for improving understanding of nuclear explosions, security forces, and transportation of nuclear materials and weapons. This category also includes $400 million in 2014 and $4 billion over the 2014–2023 period for the Office of the Administrator at the National Nuclear Security Administration.

portion of the budget: weapons activities, naval reactors, and the Office of the Administrator.

In addition to the costs directly attributable to nuclear forces, other activities are sometimes included in total nuclear costs, including dismantling retired nuclear weapons and cleaning up contamination at shuttered nuclear sites (so-called legacy costs), reducing threats

posed by nuclear proliferation and complying with arms control agreements (including monitoring the compliance of other parties to those agreements), and building and operating missile defense and other defenses against nuclear weapons from other countries. Taken together, those activities would cost about $215 billion over the next 10 years, according to CBO's estimates (see Box 1).

Box 1.

Other Nuclear-Related Costs

In addition to showing the direct costs of operating, maintaining, and modernizing U.S. nuclear forces, some studies of nuclear costs include other activities that are related to the full life-cycle cost of nuclear weapons or that play a role in determining the size of the nuclear arsenal. Those other nuclear-related costs include legacy costs of nuclear weapons, costs of threat reduction and arms control, and costs of missile defense and other defenses. To estimate those costs, the Congressional Budget Office (CBO) analyzed the budgets of the Department of Defense (DoD) and the Department of Energy (DOE) using an approach similar to the one it used to estimate the costs of nuclear forces but including costs that occur under two other appropriation titles from DOE: defense nuclear nonproliferation (part of the budget for the National Nuclear Security Administration, or NNSA), and environmental and other defense activities (part of the larger DOE budget).[1]

Legacy Costs of Nuclear Weapons

Over the next 10 years, CBO estimates, DOE's budget will include about $74 billion for nuclear weapons legacy costs, comprising $67 billion in funds for environmental and other defense activities to clean up nuclear weapons facilities; $3 billion in

---

1. CBO's estimates are based on the discretionary portion of the agencies' budgets (which is provided and controlled by annual appropriation acts) and do not include some legacy costs of nuclear weapons that receive mandatory funding.

funds for the weapons activities account to dismantle weapons and to contribute to pensions for contractors to address legacy issues; and $4 billion in funds for defense nuclear nonproliferation to dispose of fissile materials and contribute to legacy contractor pensions (see the table on the next page).[2] DOE's 2014 budget documents do not provide any projected amounts beyond 2014 for environmental and other defense activities; NNSA's budget documents provide projected amounts through 2018. For years beyond those for which budget information is available, CBO projected costs under the assumption that those activities would continue at a constant level and their costs would increase with inflation.

Costs of Threat Reduction and Arms Control

The combined plans of DoD and DOE for threat reduction and arms control will cost about $34 billion over the next decade, CBO estimates ($17 billion for DoD and $17 billion for DOE). DoD's costs in this category support some of the activities of the Defense Threat Reduction Agency, the Cooperative Threat Reduction program for securing nuclear weapons and materials in other countries,

---

2. For both weapons activities and defense nuclear nonproliferation, legacy contractor pensions represent DOE's contribution to the University of California Retirement Program for employees and annuitants of the university who worked at the Los Alamos and Lawrence Livermore national laboratories while the university was responsible for operating the labs for DOE. Those labs are now operated by different organizations.

Continued

Strategic Nuclear Forces

The United States' nuclear deterrence strategy, developed during the Cold War, is built around the strategic nuclear triad, with each leg of the triad designed to serve a particular role that complements the other legs. Bombers provide the most flexibility, because the tempo of their operations can be ramped up or down, signaling intent to an adversary. Intercontinental ballistic missiles provide the most rapid response, and their dispersed underground silos present several hundred targets that an adversary

would need to destroy if it was tempted to attack U.S. nuclear forces.[4] (By contrast, U.S. bomber bases, SSBN bases, and command-and-control facilities present a much smaller set of targets.) The ability of ballistic

---

4. Current U.S. ICBMs are fired from silos (one ICBM per silo) that are placed far apart from one another and are hardened against nuclear attack. An adversary would need to target one or more nuclear weapons at each silo to ensure destruction of the ICBM force.

Box 1.   Continued

Other Nuclear-Related Costs

Costs of Other Nuclear-Related Activities

(Billions of dollars)

Category	2014	Total, 2014 to 2023
Legacy Costs of Nuclear Weapons	7.0	74
Costs of Threat Reduction and Arms Control	3.2	34
Costs of Missile Defense and Other Defenses	10.6	107
Total	20.8	215

Source: Congressional Budget Office based on information from the Department of Defense and the Department of Energy.

Note: The table reflects budgeted amounts for the departments of Defense and Energy. It does not include potential cost growth.

on-site inspections by the military services and other activities to implement arms control agreements, and various programs that conduct research to better understand nuclear threats from other countries. DOE's costs (which will all be paid under the appropriation title for defense nuclear nonproliferation) support research related to the nonproliferation of arms and technologies to verify arms control, the Global Threat Reduction Initiative (a program for securing nuclear materials worldwide), and other activities. To project costs beyond 2018, CBO assumed that those activities would continue at a constant level and their costs would increase with inflation.

Costs of Missile Defense and Other Defenses

DoD will spend about $107 billion through 2023 to execute its plans for nuclear-related defenses, CBO estimates. Almost all of that amount ($105 billion) will support ballistic missile defense; the remainder

will support some force protection activities related to nuclear, biological, and chemical weapons. Missile defense costs include all activities of the Missile Defense Agency; the Army's costs associated with missile defense, including the Terminal High-Altitude Area Defense and Patriot missile defense systems; and 10 percent of the Navy's costs associated with procuring, maintaining, and operating the guided missile destroyers and cruisers that are capable of performing missile defense. (Missile defense is only one of multiple missions that those ships perform, and the 10 percent scaling factor reflects CBO's estimate of the fraction of time and costs that missile defense would represent in their overall mission.) CBO's cost projections beyond 2018 are based primarily on information available from DoD (such as Selected Acquisition Reports for certain programs and the Navy's 30-year shipbuilding plan) and from CBO's understanding of DoD's long-term goals for individual programs.

missile submarines to remain on alert, submerged, and undetectable for long periods makes them the most survivable of the legs, ensuring the ability of the United States to retaliate against a nuclear attack; that ability helps provide stability during a crisis and helps deter adversaries by assuring mutual destruction.

Historically, the strategic nuclear triad has formed the core of U.S. nuclear forces; over the past several decades, the centrality of the triad to U.S. nuclear strategy has

grown as tactical (short-range) nuclear forces have been reduced to a small fraction of their peak size, and intermediate-range nuclear forces have been eliminated altogether by treaty.[5] The 2010 Nuclear Posture Review restated DoD's intention to retain all three legs of the

---

5. In the Intermediate-Range Nuclear Forces Treaty, which entered into force in 1988, the United States and Soviet Union agreed to destroy all of their ground-launched ballistic and cruise missiles with ranges between 500 and 5,500 kilometers.

strategic triad. In addition to DoD's funding of the delivery systems for the triad, DOE provides support for the nuclear weapons that the bombers, ICBMs, and submarines carry and for the nuclear reactors that power those submarines.[6]

CBO estimates that DoD and DOE will need about $156 billion over the next 10 years to support the strategic nuclear triad ($132 billion for DoD and $25 billion for DOE) under the Administration's current plans, not including historical cost growth (see Table 2). Of that total, $82 billion will be allocated to SSBNs and their nuclear power reactors, missiles, and warheads; $24 billion will be allocated to ICBMs and their warheads; $40 billion will pay for strategic bombers and their nuclear armaments; and $11 billion will fund other activities.[7]

In recent months, several high-level current and former DoD officials have questioned whether the United States will be able to continue to field all of the legs of the nuclear triad in the face of mounting budgetary pressure. That concern is driven primarily by the age of the current force and the costs associated with modernizing the weapons and delivery systems. During the Cold War, systems were routinely retired to make way for new, more capable replacements. However, the current generation of systems has continued with the same primary design for decades, undergoing periodic refurbishments and upgrades: The first Minuteman III ICBMs entered service in 1970, the first Ohio class SSBN was commissioned in 1981, the first B-52H bombers were built in the early 1960s, and the B-2 bomber first flew in 1989.

Under the Administration's plans, modernization programs for all three legs of the triad would receive at least some funding within the 10-year period (2014 to 2023) considered in this report. Specifically, the following weapons and systems would be developed or modernized:

- A new ballistic missile submarine (referred to variously as the Sea-Based Strategic Deterrent, Ohio class replacement, or SSBN(X)), would be developed, along

with the nuclear reactor for its propulsion (which would be partially funded by DOE). In addition, the Trident II missiles carried on SSBNs are currently undergoing a life-extension program (LEP). The warheads carried by those missiles would also be refurbished by extending the life of the W76 warhead (which is well under way); modernizing the arming, fuzing, and firing apparatus on the W88 warhead (referred to as the W88 Alteration 370); and beginning new LEPs that would produce the interoperable warheads IW-1 and IW-2 (to replace W88 warheads), which would be capable of operating on both submarine-launched ballistic missiles and ICBMs.[8]

- A new ICBM (referred to as the Ground-Based Strategic Deterrent) would be developed, and LEPs would be put in place for the existing Minuteman III (to enable operation through 2030), the interoperable IW-1 warhead that would replace W78 warheads carried by ICBMs, and the interoperable IW-2 warhead that would replace W87 ICBM warheads.[9]

- A new bomber (referred to as the Long-Range Strike Bomber, or LRS-B) would be developed, as would the Long-Range Standoff (LRSO) weapon (to replace the Air-Launched Cruise Missile, or ALCM, carried by the B-52H bomber and to add cruise-missile capability to the B-2 bomber). Two LEPs would be implemented, one for the B61 bomb carried on bombers and one for the warhead chosen to be carried on the new Long-Range Standoff weapon.[10]

---

6. DOE also supports nuclear power reactors used by aircraft carriers and submarines other than SSBNs, but those activities do not support nuclear forces and their costs are not considered in this report.

7. "Other activities" in this case refers primarily to base support and DoD's research related to nuclear forces that CBO was unable to directly attribute to one of the legs of the triad.

8. The fuze is the portion of the weapon that originates the signal that triggers the firing system.

9. DoD is analyzing alternatives to determine how to fulfill the ICBM mission after 2030. For this study, CBO assumed that DoD would develop a new silo-based missile similar to the Minuteman III. Design of that missile would need to begin around 2018 to ensure that the new missile was available by 2030. DoD is also considering other options, some of which would cost less than a new ICBM similar to the Minuteman, and some of which would cost more.

10. The B61 has several versions; some are carried on strategic bombers and others on tactical aircraft. Current plans call for most of those versions to be combined into a single version that can be used for strategic and tactical missions as part of the life-extension program. In addition, DoD and DOE are analyzing alternatives to determine which of the existing warhead types the new cruise missile will carry. Once that choice is made, the selected warhead will undergo modernization to extend its life.

Costs to Operate, Sustain, and Modernize the Triad.
CBO analyzed the costs of operating, sustaining, and modernizing strategic nuclear forces.[11] For that analysis, CBO used the following definitions:

- *Operations* includes all of DoD's operation and support costs directly related to the nuclear triad—that is, all costs under the appropriations for operation and maintenance and for military personnel.

- *Sustainment* includes all of DoD's acquisition costs—that is, all costs under the appropriations for procurement and for RDT&E—for existing weapon delivery systems (except for major life-extension programs for those systems), as well as DOE's costs for sustaining the relevant warhead types and supporting naval reactors on current SSBNs.

- *Modernization* includes all of DoD's acquisition costs for major life-extension programs for existing systems and costs for new systems that would replace the current delivery systems. This category also includes DOE's costs for LEPs for the relevant types of warheads and for development of the reactor for the new SSBN.

DoD's and DOE's combined costs to support the strategic triad will be about $9.8 billion in 2014, CBO estimates: $4.2 billion for operations, $2.2 billion for sustainment of current systems, and $3.3 billion for modernization.[12] CBO expects the cost of the triad to grow sharply after 2014 because of the many modernization programs that will be under way for all three legs of the triad (see Figure 1). By 2023, the annual cost for the triad is estimated to rise to $17.1 billion, an increase of about 75 percent over the 2014 amount, with $5.4 billion for operations, $2.1 billion for sustainment of current systems, and $9.7 billion for modernization.[13] The highest single-year cost during the 2014–2023 period is projected

to occur in 2022, when the Navy is slated to still be paying for the first of the new SSBNs and beginning advance procurement on the second submarine.[14] The total cost for the triad will be $20.8 billion in that year, more than double the 2014 amount.

The cost of modernization will grow throughout the 10-year projection period, accounting for 50 percent of the total cost of the triad by 2019; annual modernization costs are likely to remain high beyond 2023. Many of the programs listed above will be in their early stages of development before 2023, so most of their costs will occur after the 10-year period that CBO examined. The Navy plans to procure the first of the new SSBNs (and begin advance procurement for a second) within the 10-year period but will procure the remaining 10 submarines, at a rate of one submarine each year, starting in 2026. In addition, under current plans, two new modernization efforts will begin sometime after 2023: a replacement for the Trident II D-5 ballistic missile carried by SSBNs, and a LEP for the SSBN-borne W76 warhead that would add cross-platform capability and result in a third interoperable warhead (IW-3). During the period from 2024 to 2030, when DOE would continue to perform LEPs on several types of warheads and DoD would concurrently purchase new versions of the SSBN, ICBM, and strategic bomber, the cost of modernization would average about $15 billion per year, CBO estimates, or more than four times the 2014 amount. Operations and sustainment costs might also grow during that period to support the staffing and maintenance of both current-generation systems and new systems during the transition to the new systems.

CBO based its estimates on the most recent detailed budget documentation available from DoD and DOE and projected future costs under the assumption that those plans would be executed successfully and on budget. Using those data, CBO estimates that the two agencies' costs for modernization programs for the triad would total about $76 billion over the next decade. (DoD's costs would account for about $58 billion of that amount.)

---

11. CBO's estimates of the costs of the triad include only those costs that can be directly associated with the delivery systems and weapons of the triad; they exclude DoD's costs for command, control, communications, and early warning and DOE's costs for nuclear weapons laboratories and supporting activities.

12. That total excludes costs of some research and operational support activities for strategic nuclear forces that CBO was unable to associate with a specific type of delivery system.

13. The increase in total costs for the triad from 2014 to 2023 will be about 45 percent in real terms (with the effects of inflation removed), CBO estimates.

14. According to the Navy's Fiscal Year 2014 Shipbuilding Plan, the first new SSBN will be bought in 2021, and the full cost of the ship (minus any amounts funded in advance) will be funded in that year. However, CBO expects that the Navy will request permission to spread the cost of each ship over several years (through incremental funding), as it has done with some other classes of large ships, like aircraft carriers. That approach is reflected in CBO's estimate.

Figure 1.

Budgets for Operating, Sustaining, and Modernizing the Strategic Nuclear Triad

(Billions of dollars)

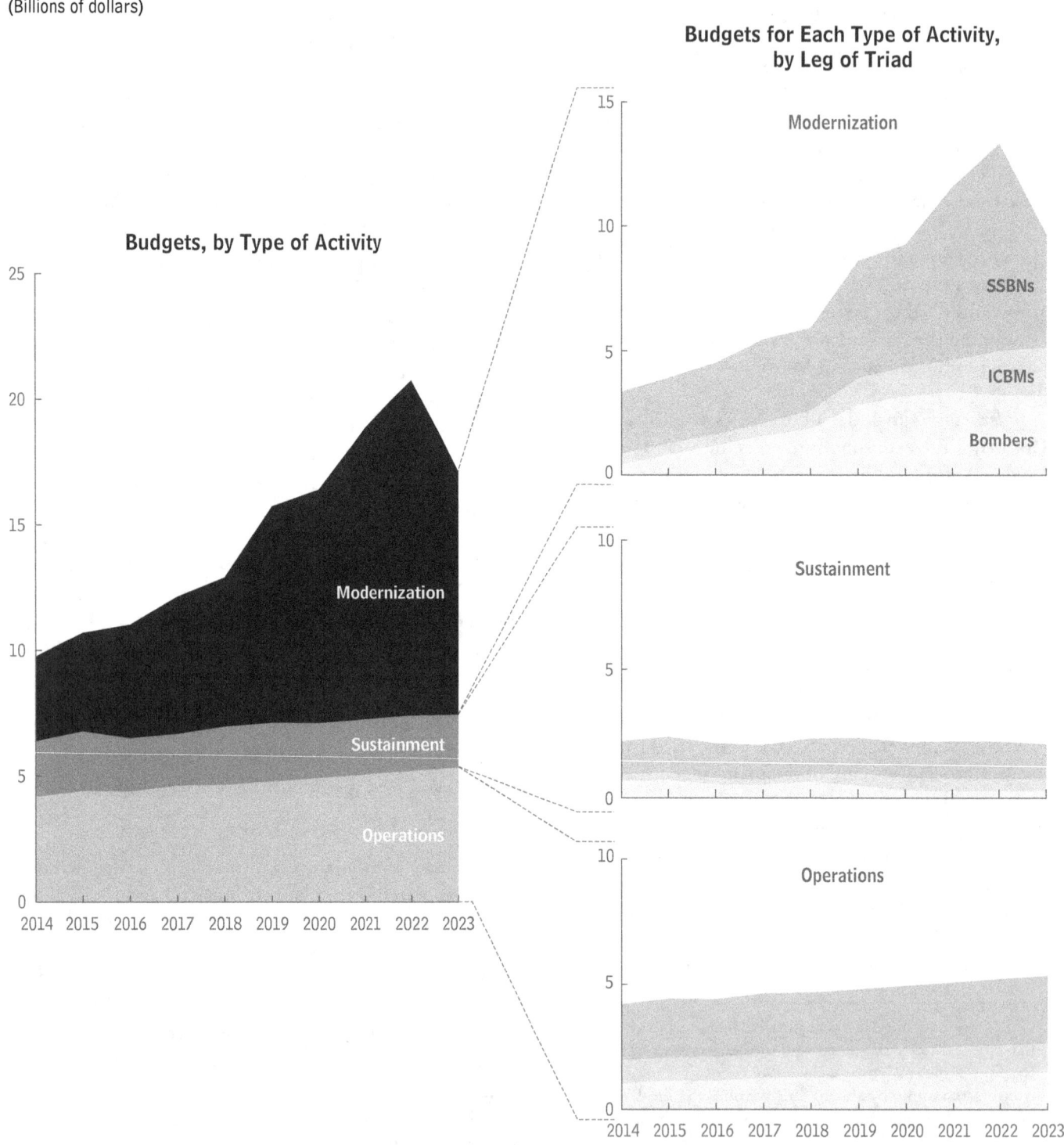

Source: Congressional Budget Office based on information from the Department of Defense (DoD) and the Department of Energy (DOE).

Notes: The figure reflects budgeted amounts for the departments of Defense and Energy. It does not include potential cost growth. CBO's
estimates of the costs of the triad only include those costs that can be directly associated with the delivery systems and weapons of
the triad; they exclude DoD's costs for command, control, communications, and early warning and DOE's costs for nuclear weapons
laboratories and supporting activities.

SSBN = ballistic missile submarine; ICBM = intercontinental ballistic missile.

Historically, however, many development programs for new systems have experienced technical difficulties that led to cost growth. Because cost growth is often manifested in delays in program schedules as well as growth in annual costs, though, some cost growth might be shifted outside the 10-year period if work was deferred beyond 2023.

Comparing Costs for the Legs of the Triad. Under current plans, costs would increase for each leg of the strategic triad over the next decade, CBO estimates. Costs for the SSBN leg would increase from $6.0 billion in 2014 to $8.5 billion in 2023, reaching a peak of $12.4 billion in 2022, when the purchase of the first two new SSBNs would be occurring; costs for the ICBM leg would rise from $1.6 billion in 2014 to $3.6 billion in 2023; and for the bomber leg, costs would increase from $2.2 billion in 2014 to $5.0 billion in 2023 (see Figure 2).

The cost of SSBNs will be substantially higher than that of the other two legs from 2014 to 2023, accounting for 56 percent of the total, CBO estimates. (Bombers will account for 27 percent of the total cost; and ICBMs, 17 percent.) SSBNs are expensive to purchase and operate given the complex nature of the submarines themselves, and the national security strategy calls for multiple SSBNs to be deployed at sea and on alert at all times. In addition, the need to perform periodic maintenance on the submarines, to train the crews, to spend time transiting from their bases to alert stations, and for some submarines at the bases to be prepared to deploy on short notice in a crisis means the Navy must maintain a fleet of submarines several times larger than the number of SSBNs that DoD plans to keep at sea and on alert at a given time.

However, the relative cost of each leg of the triad depends strongly on how much of the cost of bombers is attributed to the nuclear mission. CBO applied 25 percent of the costs associated with the B-52H bomber and 100 percent of the costs associated with the B-2 bomber to the nuclear mission. (For additional discussion, see "Basis of CBO's Estimates" on page 18.) CBO also applied the 25 percent apportionment factor to costs associated with the new Long-Range Strike Bomber, under the assumption that DoD would use the new bomber in a manner roughly similar to the way it now uses the B-52H. If 100 percent of the costs for the B-52H and the new bomber were included, the total estimated 10-year

cost for the three legs of the triad would increase from $145 billion to $179 billion, and the difference between the costs of the SSBN and bomber legs would be narrowed substantially. (SSBNs would average 46 percent of the total, and bombers would average 41 percent.)

Another factor that affects the relative cost of the legs of the triad is how costs are apportioned between SSBNs and ICBMs for the life-extension programs that are expected to produce the new interoperable warheads. One approach would be to split the costs according to the total number of warheads for each leg. That was not possible, however, because the inventory for each type of warhead is classified. Thus, for this report, CBO has split the cost evenly between SSBNs and ICBMs for the first and second interoperable warheads (IW-1 and IW-2).

Caution should be taken in using the costs in this report to estimate savings from a cut to nuclear forces. Because of fixed costs for infrastructure and other factors, a partial reduction in the size of the force from cuts to any of the current systems that make up the nuclear triad would be likely to result in cost savings that were proportionally less than the relative reduction in the force. (For example, fielding half as many Minuteman III ICBMs—cutting from the current 450 to 225—would reduce costs somewhat, but the resulting costs would probably still be more than half of the projected amounts under the current plan.) Completely eliminating a leg of the nuclear triad would generate substantial savings, but it would also incur costs to retire the systems involved and to decommission the associated facilities, which would reduce the net savings, at least temporarily. Furthermore, full savings from such a cut would only be realized if the military positions associated with the systems were eliminated (as opposed to being assigned to other tasks.) Conversely, the potential savings in *life-cycle* costs from eliminating a leg of the triad (and the associated military personnel) would probably be higher than the costs shown in this report, because the 10-year period examined here does not capture the full cost of modernizing nuclear forces. For each leg of the triad, most of the cost to procure new systems would occur after 2023.

SSBNs. Of the $82 billion cost for the SSBN leg through 2023, CBO estimates that $71 billion would fund DoD's activities and $11 billion would fund DOE's activities, including $6 billion for weapons activities and $4 billion

Figure 2.

Budgets for Legs of the Strategic Nuclear Triad

(Billions of dollars)

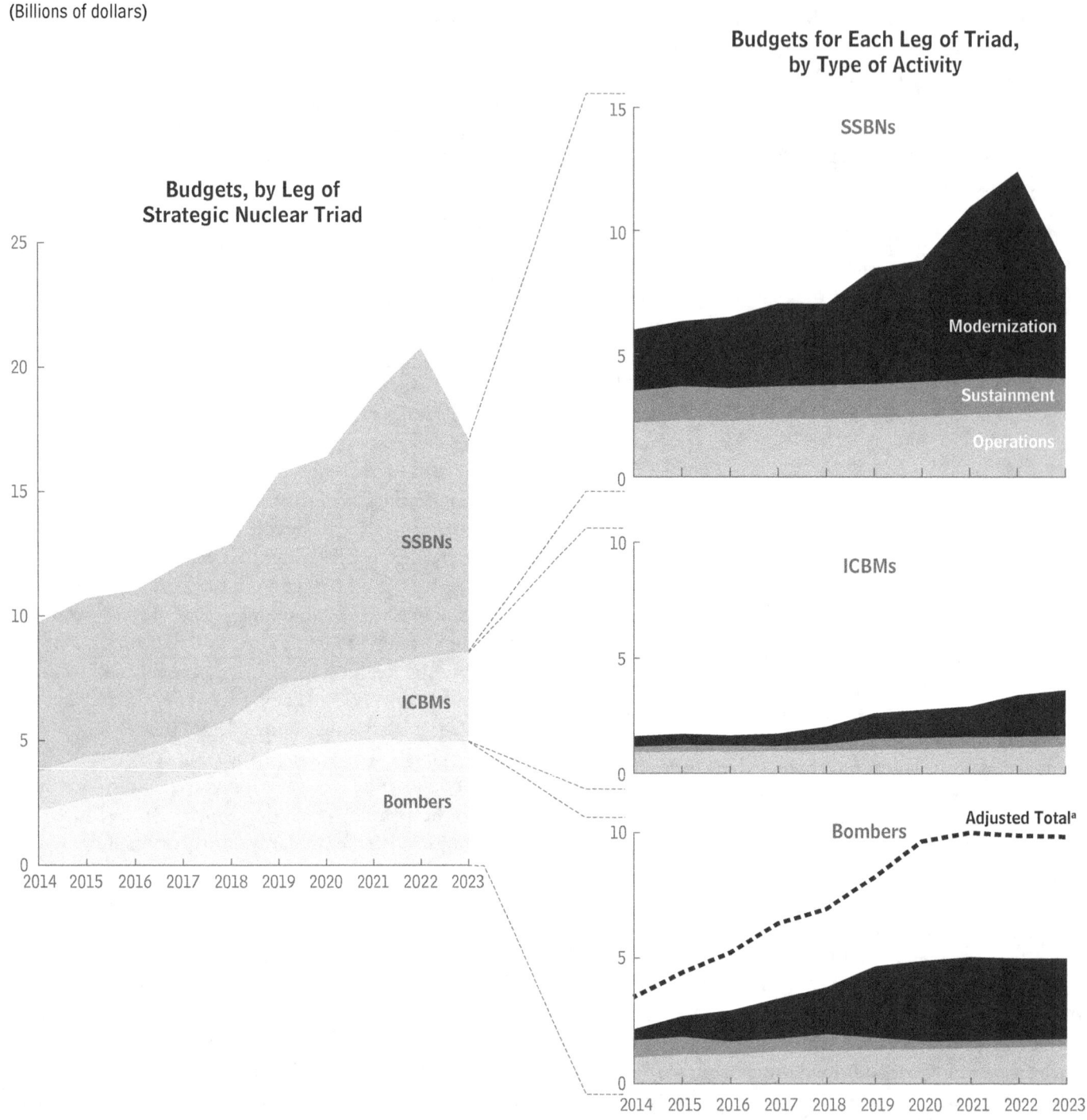

Source: Congressional Budget Office based on information from the Department of Defense (DoD) and the Department of Energy (DOE).

Notes: The figure reflects budgeted amounts for the departments of Defense and Energy. It does not include potential cost growth. CBO's estimates of the costs of the triad only include those costs that can be directly associated with the delivery systems and weapons of the triad; they exclude DoD's costs for command, control, communications, and early warning and DOE's costs for nuclear weapons laboratories and supporting activities.

SSBN = ballistic missile submarine; ICBM = intercontinental ballistic missile.

a.   The adjusted total shows the cost if 100 percent of the cost of the B-52 and the new strategic bombers was apportioned to the nuclear mission, not the 25 percent share that CBO used.

Table 3.

Budgeted Amounts for the Strategic Nuclear Triad, 2014 to 2023

(Billions of dollars)

Type of Appropriation	SSBNs	ICBMs	Bombers	Other	Total
Department of Defense					
Military personnel	6	6	3	6	20
Operation and maintenance	19	5	10	3	36
Procurement	33	2	5	0	40
Research, development, test, and evaluation	14	7	12	3	36
Subtotal	71	20	29	11	132
Department of Energy					
Weapons activities	6	4	10	n.a.	20
Naval reactors	4	n.a.	n.a.	n.a.	4
Subtotal	11	4	10	n.a.	25
Total	**82**	**24**	**40**	**11**	**156**

Source: Congressional Budget Office based on information from the Department of Defense and the Department of Energy.

Notes: The table reflects budgeted amounts for the departments of Defense and Energy, and it does not include potential cost growth. The values are based on CBO's analysis of the departments' budget proposals and accompanying documents, as well as CBO's projections of those budget figures under the assumption that programs will proceed as described in budget documentation. The category also includes several programs for which plans are still being formulated; in those cases, CBO based its estimate on historical costs of analogous programs. The budgeted amounts should not be considered independent estimates by CBO of the costs of U.S. nuclear forces.

       SSBN = ballistic missile submarine; ICBM = intercontinental ballistic missile; n.a. = not applicable.

for support of naval reactors (see Table 3).[15] Broken out another way, $38 billion of the cost would be used to operate ($24 billion) and sustain ($14 billion) the current generation of systems, whereas $44 billion would be used for modernization (see the upper right panel of Figure 2).

DoD's activities related to the current generation of systems include sustaining and operating the 14 existing Ohio class submarines (including the cost of refueling the nuclear power reactors), sustaining and operating the Trident II D-5 ballistic missiles that the submarines carry, providing base support, and instituting various RDT&E programs directly related to SSBN technology and operations. DoD's modernization activities include implementing a LEP for the D-5 ballistic missiles to extend their lifetime through 2042; refurbishing the arming, fuzing, and firing systems on the W88 warhead (DoD's portion); and developing and procuring the lead ship of a new class of submarine to replace the Ohio class.

CBO's estimate of the costs of the new SSBN is based on DoD's current plans, which call for the first submarine to be purchased in 2021.[16] CBO assumed that any funding to develop a replacement for the Trident II D-5 ballistic missile would occur after 2023.

The $6 billion for DOE's weapons activities supports current systems by sustaining the W76 and W88 warheads carried on SSBNs. It also supports modernizing other warheads by providing an ongoing LEP for the W76; funding DOE's portion of the refurbishment of the W88 arming, fuzing, and firing systems; and funding a LEP that would produce the IW-1 warhead and initial efforts on a LEP to produce the IW-2 warhead. For the costs related to DOE's naval reactors, CBO included as part of modernization 100 percent of the funds designated as pertaining to development of the reactor for the Ohio replacement submarine, and the agency included as part of sustainment 20 percent of the remainder of

---

15. Some of DOE's naval reactor activities have been paid for through transfers of budget authority from DoD to DOE. Because those activities appear in DOE's budget, CBO categorized the total naval reactor budget as belonging to DOE.

16. For more detail on the Navy's plans for the new SSBN in the context of its overall shipbuilding plans, see Congressional Budget Office, *An Analysis of the Navy's Fiscal Year 2014 Shipbuilding Plan* (October 2013), www.cbo.gov/publication/44655.

DOE's funds for naval reactors for sustaining the current Ohio class SSBN reactors. The 20 percent scaling factor reflects the ratio of the number of SSBNs to the total number of nuclear-powered ships (which also includes aircraft carriers and submarines other than SSBNs).

The largest source of uncertainty for the SSBN cost estimates through 2023 is related to the development and procurement of the new SSBN. To reduce costs in the short run, DoD decided in its 2013 budget plans to delay the procurement of the first submarine until 2021, two years later than it had previously planned. If the first submarine was further delayed, either to reduce near-term costs or because of difficulties in its development, costs within the next decade would probably be lower, although the total cost of the new SSBN would probably be higher, as has happened with other "stretched" development programs. The Navy has been looking for ways to reduce the unit cost of the new SSBN, and it remains to be seen how successful those efforts might be given the history of cost growth in DoD's development programs.

Another source of uncertainty is the cost of the recent plan to replace the W88 with the IW-1 and IW-2 warheads. Achieving cross-platform capability using existing warheads will require a complex LEP; and several nuclear experts, as well as the House Armed Services Committee, have expressed concern about the concept of interoperable warheads.[17] One of the factors contributing to that concern is the rising cost of the life-extension program for the B61, another complex LEP that will replace several different versions of that weapon with a single version. Although the B61 LEP is still in the design stage, cost estimates for the program have more than doubled from the original estimate.

ICBMs. Over the next 10 years, CBO estimates, the costs to operate, sustain, and modernize ICBMs will be $24 billion: $20 billion for DoD and $4 billion for DOE (see Table 3). Of that total, $14 billion will fund operations ($10 billion) and sustainment ($4 billion) of current systems, and $10 billion will fund modernization (see Figure 2 on page 12).

The current systems that DoD will be operating and sustaining include the Minuteman III ICBMs, helicopters used for transportation on the large ICBM bases, and other base support. DoD's modernization efforts include a LEP to extend the life of the Minuteman III until at least 2030, modernization of fuzes for ICBM warheads, and initial development of a new ICBM to replace the Minuteman III. The $4 billion in DOE funding falls in the weapons activities category. It will support sustainment of the W78 and W87 warheads and modernization (through LEPs) to integrate the W78 into the first interoperable warhead and the W87 into the second interoperable warhead.

The uncertainty in CBO's estimates of ICBM costs stems primarily from two sources. The largest source is the lack of defined plans for the new ICBM. For its analysis, CBO assumes that DoD will spend the next several years determining the best way to fulfill the future ICBM mission (a process that has already begun), choose to develop a new ICBM similar to the Minuteman III, and start to develop that new ICBM around 2018. Production of the new ICBM would occur after 2023. CBO's estimates are based on actual costs associated with Minuteman III development, adjusted for inflation and increased by 50 percent for cost growth between generations of missiles.[18] However, DoD is reportedly considering several alternatives to fulfill the ICBM mission after 2030, some of which (like another refurbishment of the Minuteman III) could cost less than the new ICBM that CBO has included in its estimate, and some of which (like a mobile ICBM) could cost more. Considerable uncertainty is also associated with the nature of the LEPs that would integrate the W78 and W87 warheads into the IW-1 and IW-2. That integration has the potential for considerable cost growth because the concept of interoperable warheads is new and because the required LEPs would be complex.

Bombers. In CBO's estimation, DoD's costs for strategic bombers will be about $29 billion over the next decade and DOE's costs will be roughly $10 billion, for a combined cost of $40 billion (see Table 3 on page 13). Of that 10-year total, $18 billion will be for operating ($13 billion) and sustaining ($5 billion) the current generation of systems, and $22 billion will be for modernizing them (see Figure 2 on page 12).

---

17. House Committee on Armed Services, *National Defense Authorization Act for Fiscal Year 2014: Report on H.R. 1960 Together with Additional and Dissenting Views,* House Report 113-102 (June 7, 2013), pp. 355–356, http://go.usa.gov/ZaH9 (PDF, 1.4 MB).

18. Historically, new weapon systems have typically cost substantially more than the systems they replace, even after adjusting for inflation.

Specifically, DoD's bomber costs are for sustaining and operating the B-52H and B-2 bombers and the Air-Launched Cruise Missile and providing base support for strategic air forces.[19] DoD's modernization efforts include designing a new tail kit for the B61 nuclear bomb that would be installed after the bombs undergo the LEP process; modernizing the B-2 defensive management system; and developing the new Long-Range Standoff weapon (to replace the ALCM) and the new Long-Range Strike Bomber.[20] CBO included in its cost estimates 25 percent of the total anticipated budgets for the B-52 and the LRS-B because that is the fraction of B-52H aircraft that concentrate on the nuclear mission at a given time, in CBO's estimation; in contrast, CBO included 100 percent of the cost of the B-2 bomber and the LRSO weapon.

All of DOE's $10 billion in bomber funding falls in the weapons activities category; that funding will support sustainment of the B83, the versions of the B61 bombs carried by strategic bombers, and the W80 warhead carried by the Air-Launched Cruise Missile. Through the life-extension program, that funding will also support modernization of the B61 and of the warhead type (yet to be determined) for the new LRSO cruise missile. Current plans for the B61 LEP would replace most of the various versions of that bomb—some of which are carried by strategic bombers and some of which are carried by tactical aircraft—with a single version, the B61-12, capable of being carried by both types of aircraft. On the basis of those plans, CBO included half of the estimated cost of the B61 LEP in the strategic bomber category and half in the tactical forces category.[21]

As noted, CBO's estimates incorporate the assessment that approximately 25 percent of the costs of the B-52H and the new bomber can be attributed to the nuclear mission (see "Basis of CBO's Estimates" on page 18 for more details). Other studies have used different

apportionment factors, some as high as 100 percent. If CBO had included 100 percent of the costs for the B-52H ($12 billion) and the new bomber ($32 billion) instead of 25 percent, the total estimated cost of strategic bombers through 2023 would have increased to about $73 billion, almost twice CBO's estimate in the current analysis (see Figure 2 on page 12).

As with the other two legs of the triad, the lack of firm modernization plans creates uncertainty in CBO's estimate of bomber costs. Concept development for the LRSO cruise missile is ongoing: DoD's budget documents call for development of the systems to begin around 2015. CBO assumed that development would continue beyond 2023 and that procurement would not occur until after that. CBO used the actual costs of developing the ALCM as a basis for projecting budgets for the LRSO weapon beyond 2018. Concept development for the Long-Range Strike Bomber is also ongoing; to project budgets beyond 2018, CBO used the cost analysis described in a previous CBO report.[22] CBO assumed that procurement of the new bomber would begin in 2022, consistent with DoD's statements indicating the new bomber would be operational in the mid-2020s. If DoD pursued concepts or schedules that differed from those used by CBO to estimate the costs, actual costs would diverge from CBO's estimates, perhaps substantially.

The B61 LEP is another source of uncertainty in CBO's estimate. DOE's estimate of the cost of the B61 LEP has increased significantly in recent years, from a total of about $4 billion in the 2012 Stockpile Stewardship Management Plan to about $7 billion in the 2014 version of that plan. However, an independent cost estimate for the B61 LEP performed by DoD in the summer of 2012 said the total cost could be as high as $10 billion. CBO's estimate of costs over the next decade for the bomber portion of the B61 LEP is about $3 billion (half of the total B61 LEP costs during that period, split with tactical forces), not including cost growth at historical rates; actual costs would be higher if DoD's estimate proved to be correct, although how much of that increase would occur within the 2014–2023 period is uncertain.[23]

---

19. Although the B-1 bomber was originally designed to be nuclear-capable, it no longer has a nuclear mission and is not included in CBO's estimate.

20. The tail kit allows the bomb to maneuver after leaving the bomber, thus improving the accuracy of the bomb.

21. An alternate approach would split the costs between tactical and strategic missions according to the number of warheads of each type the B61-12 would replace. However, the number of warheads of any given type in the U.S. arsenal is classified, so for this analysis CBO has split the cost evenly between the two types of missions.

22. Congressional Budget Office, *Alternatives for Long-Range Ground-Attack Systems* (March 2006), pp. 37–55, www.cbo.gov/publication/17686.

23. CBO's 10-year estimate is less than the full cost of the program because it does not include sunk costs before 2014 (which total about $400 million) or costs beyond 2023 (about $500 million in the 2014 Stockpile Stewardship Management Plan).

Tactical Nuclear Forces

The United States maintains the ability to deploy nuclear weapons on short-range aircraft. Although the United States has reduced its number of forward-deployed weapons, it still fields a "small number" of nuclear weapons in Europe in support of the North Atlantic Treaty Organization (NATO).[24] Two types of U.S. tactical aircraft, the Air Force's F-16 and F-15E, are capable of carrying nuclear weapons; plans call for the Air Force's F-35A to also be nuclear-capable. Those aircraft carry versions of the B61 bomb.

The cost of U.S. tactical nuclear forces will total about $7 billion over the next 10 years, CBO estimates, about $4 billion of which is for DoD and the rest of which is for DOE. Activities supported by DoD consist of sustaining and operating the F-16 and F-15E aircraft, sustaining and operating storage systems for theater nuclear weapons, and supporting NATO. DoD's modernization efforts include developing nuclear capability for the F-35 aircraft, which is not yet operational. All of the $3 billion for DOE falls in the weapons activities category, which supports sustainment of the tactical versions of the B61 and the planned B61 LEP. Because the new version of the B61 will have both strategic and tactical missions, half of the total cost of the B61 LEP has been attributed to the tactical nuclear mission.

Estimating the total cost for tactical nuclear weapons involves considerable uncertainty because of the limited information available about the fraction of costs of tactical delivery systems that can be attributed to the nuclear mission and because of the potential for growth in the cost of the B61 LEP. In addition, the number and location of U.S. nuclear weapons in Europe are classified, which makes it difficult to assess the level of effort required to maintain them.

For this report, CBO assumed that 10 percent of the costs for military personnel and for operation and maintenance associated with F-16 and F-15E aircraft could be attributed to the nuclear mission, which includes the cost to support forward-deployed aircraft and the cost to maintain nuclear certification of the aircraft and their crews. No procurement or RDT&E costs for those aircraft were included because CBO assumed that no

upgrades or additional aircraft would be required to continue the nuclear mission.

Similarly, CBO did not include any procurement costs for the F-35 (which will replace the F-16), because the agency assumed that no additional aircraft would be required to accomplish the nuclear mission. On the basis of information provided by DoD, CBO estimates that it would cost about $350 million to finish developing the modifications to make the F-35 nuclear-capable. The plan for implementing those modifications on aircraft is still being developed, so no costs for that implementation have been included in CBO's estimate of costs for the next 10 years.

The forward-deployed nuclear weapons in Europe are fielded as part of U.S. support to NATO, which determines nuclear strategy through its Nuclear Planning Group. CBO included 20 percent of the costs of the Air Force's support to NATO but included none of the NATO support costs of the other services.

Nuclear Weapons Laboratories

The cost of DOE's plans for laboratory activities and infrastructure to support its nuclear weapons capability will be about $101 billion over the next decade, CBO estimates.[25] That total includes about $24 billion for activities unique to specific warhead types ($5 billion for sustainment and $19 billion for life-extension programs), which CBO included in the strategic and tactical categories of costs. Of the remaining $77 billion, $73 billion is under the weapons activities appropriation title, and $4 billion is under the Office of the Administrator appropriation title in NNSA's budget.[26]

Within the weapons activities appropriation title, costs that DOE directly associates with sustaining or modernizing nuclear warheads are contained in the subcategory

---

24. Department of Defense, *Nuclear Posture Review Report* (April 2010), p. xii, http://go.usa.gov/ZaM4 (PDF, 2.7 MB).

25. DOE's costs under the naval reactors appropriation title are not included in these totals; the portion of those costs relevant to nuclear weapons and forces, about $4 billion, was included in the totals for SSBNs instead. When added to the $101 billion for nuclear weapons laboratories and infrastructure, the total DOE budget for nuclear forces is $105 billion, as shown in Table 2 on page 5.

26. CBO categorized the budget for weapons dismantlement and payments for legacy contractor pensions (which falls under the weapons activities appropriation title) as related to legacy nuclear weapons costs and thus included that budget in the costs of other nuclear-related activities for this report.

of Directed Stockpile Work. About 60 percent of the budget for Directed Stockpile Work is associated with sustaining or modernizing specific warhead types; CBO grouped those costs with the costs of their associated delivery systems. Nearly all of the remaining 40 percent of the budget for that subcategory covers stockpile services, which are activities that directly support the capability and production capacity to sustain and modernize warheads but that are not unique to a specific warhead type.[27] Those services include developing and certifying the manufacturing process, handling special nuclear materials, calibrating and certifying tools and test equipment, and supporting processes used on more than a single type of warhead. For this analysis, CBO grouped stockpile services with the rest of the costs for DOE's nuclear laboratory complex.

Of the $73 billion in costs for weapons activities, $30 billion is for infrastructure ($18 billion for site stewardship, which includes operations of laboratory facilities and small construction projects, and $12 billion for nuclear programs, which covers the production and handling of special nuclear materials, such as uranium and plutonium, and also includes several large construction projects for new facilities to support that mission); $12 billion is for stockpile services; and $31 billion is for various research and support activities intended to enable DOE to sustain and modernize nuclear warheads in the future.[28] Spending for those research and support activities consists of $7 billion for advanced simulation and computing; $7 billion for defense nuclear security (including the physical security of facilities, cybersecurity, and secure accountability for nuclear materials); $5 billion for science programs (research to understand how materials behave under extreme conditions, which will be used to support stockpile assessments, certification of nuclear weapon components, and other missions); and $13 billion that will be distributed among several other categories.

---

27. About 2 percent of the budget for Directed Stockpile Work covers weapons dismantlement, which CBO grouped with the cost of legacy nuclear weapons.

28. Plans call for DoD to transfer about $7 billion in budget authority to NNSA between 2014 and 2018 to support various weapons activities, including infrastructure modernization. Because those activities appear in DOE's budget, CBO categorized the full weapons activities budget as belonging to DOE.

If they follow historical trends, efforts related to sustaining and modernizing the weapons stockpile are likely to be particularly susceptible to cost growth. NNSA's budget for weapons activities in its fiscal year 2014 submission is about 10 percent higher than the amount in its fiscal year 2013 submission ($34 billion compared with $31 billion) for 2014 through 2017 (the period over which the two submissions overlap). That difference is driven primarily by an increase in the expected costs to sustain and modernize weapons, although costs for other supporting activities also grew. In recent years, several construction projects have experienced substantial cost growth relative to their initial estimates; for example, in the 2013 budget submission, the decision was made to defer construction for at least five years on the Chemistry and Metallurgy Research Replacement Nuclear Facility because of increasing costs. The Government Accountability Office (GAO) has published several reports that address actual or potential cost growth in NNSA's major projects, particularly construction projects and warhead LEPs, and NNSA has several additional major construction projects and warhead LEPs planned over the coming years.[29]

Nuclear Command, Control, Communications, and Early-Warning Systems

The abilities to communicate with nuclear forces, issue commands that tightly control their use, and detect incoming attacks (or ascertain that no attack is coming) are critical for effective and safe use of nuclear weapons and their delivery systems. DoD plans to spend about $56 billion over the next 10 years for command, control, communications, and early-warning systems for the nuclear mission, CBO estimates.

DoD fields many of those types of systems, most of which are used by both nuclear and conventional forces. The portion of costs for those systems that stems from the nuclear mission is uncertain. Instead of attempting to estimate the fraction of nuclear-related use for each system, CBO included costs for only those systems that the agency judged to be the most critical to the use of nuclear forces (should such an occasion arise) and attributed all of

---

29. Government Accountability Office, *Nuclear Weapons: NNSA and DOD Need to More Effectively Manage the Stockpile Life Extension Program*, GAO-09-385 (March 2009), www.gao.gov/products/ GAO-09-385, and *Department of Energy: Major Construction Projects Need a Consistent Approach for Assessing Technology Readiness to Help Avoid Cost Increases and Delays*, GAO-07-336 (March 2007), www.gao.gov/products/GAO-07-336.

the costs for those systems to the nuclear mission. For example, CBO included 100 percent of the costs for satellite communications systems using "protected" frequencies—the Milstar, Advanced Extremely High Frequency, and Polar MILSATCOM satellites—and none of the costs for other satellite communications systems, such as Wideband Global SATCOM. (The systems that use protected frequencies are designed to be the most secure and survivable in the event of a nuclear exchange.)

Another source of uncertainty in CBO's estimates is the potential for new modernization activities that are not yet reflected in DoD's budget. CBO's estimates incorporate costs associated with several ongoing modernization programs for communications and early-warning systems, including the transition from the Defense Support Program satellites for detecting missile launches to the Space-Based Infrared System, the transition from Milstar to Advanced Extremely High Frequency satellites, and upgrades to radars for the Ballistic Missile Early Warning System.[30] However, press reports indicate that other modernization programs may be needed, in particular for the command and control of nuclear forces; costs for those programs are not yet reflected in DoD's budget or CBO's estimates.[31]

Command and Control. The cost of executing DoD's plans over the next decade will include about $13 billion for command-and-control activities related to nuclear forces, in CBO's estimation. That total comprises costs associated with the primary nuclear-related commands (U.S. Strategic Command, or STRATCOM, and the North American Aerospace Defense Command, or NORAD), including headquarters costs, support to those commands by the service branches, and strategic planning activities; the National Military Command Center; and the National Airborne Operations Center aircraft.

Communications. Through 2023, DoD plans to spend about $23 billion to support communications systems critical to the nuclear mission. Supported systems include

the communications portion of Fleet Ballistic Missile Control; the Minimum Essential Emergency Communications Network; the Family of Advanced Beyond-Line-of-Sight Terminals; and Milstar, Polar MILSATCOM, and Advanced Extremely High Frequency satellites.

Early-Warning Systems. CBO estimates that DoD will allocate about $20 billion to support the following early-warning systems between 2014 and 2023: the Atmospheric Early Warning System, the Ballistic Missile Early Warning System, the Submarine-Launched Ballistic Missile Radar Warning System, the Space-Based Infrared System, and nuclear detection sensors carried as secondary payloads on several conventional satellite systems (for example, Global Positioning System satellites).

Basis of CBO's Estimates

CBO based its cost estimates for the nuclear enterprise on the 2014 budgets of the Department of Defense and the Department of Energy and their associated detailed budget justification documents. Each department typically projects budgets for four years beyond the upcoming budget year. CBO also used the 2014 version of the Stockpile Stewardship Management Plan from DOE's National Nuclear Security Administration to prepare its cost estimates.

CBO's Approach

CBO analyzed DoD's and DOE's budgets line by line to identify activities associated with nuclear weapons. For budget lines that include both nuclear and nonnuclear activities, CBO estimated the fraction of costs associated with nuclear activities. For B-52H bombers, for example, CBO estimated that 25 percent of the total costs of B-52Hs arise from their nuclear mission because, even though all B-52H aircraft are nuclear-capable, only about 25 percent of them are dedicated to the nuclear mission at a given time, in CBO's estimation.[32]

---

30. Upgrades to radars for the Ballistic Missile Early Warning System (to improve the system's overall performance and enhance its utility for ballistic missile defense) are funded through the Missile Defense Agency; for this report, those funds are included in the other nuclear-related category (instead of the nuclear forces category), along with other missile defense activities.

31. Christopher J. Castelli, "DNI Reviewing STRATCOM Panel's Call for New NIE on Nuclear C2," *Inside Missile Defense* (November 14, 2012), p. 5.

32. Press reports indicate that one of the four Air Force B-52H squadrons is focused specifically on the nuclear mission, with personnel and aircraft rotating through that squadron. See, for example, Marcus Weisgerber, "USAF to Activate Rotational Nuclear Bomber Squadron Next Month," *Inside the Air Force* (September 26, 2008). Current plans for compliance with the New START treaty call for some B-52H aircraft to be converted to purely conventional missions by removing their nuclear capability, but CBO has assumed that those conversions would not change the number of aircraft dedicated to the nuclear role at a given time.

To produce 10-year estimates, CBO projected each budget line beyond the five years available in the departments' documents by examining the long-range plans for each program. For replacement systems that are expected to begin development within the 2014–2023 period but are not yet fully reflected in the departments' budgets (specifically, the Long-Range Strike Bomber, the new cruise missile, and the future ICBM), CBO estimated the costs of those systems by reviewing actual costs for analogous systems that have already been built and the schedules that would be required to keep inventories at planned levels. Many of CBO's projections also draw on analyses done for other CBO reports.[33]

For operation and maintenance activities and the number of military personnel, CBO used the planned 2018 levels for subsequent years as well. In keeping with DoD's historical experience, CBO projects that costs for those categories will grow somewhat faster than inflation.[34]

For research, development, and procurement, CBO projected costs for individual programs on the basis of the available budgetary and program data and did not attempt to quantify additional cost growth—that is, increases in costs as programs evolve that exceed the amounts anticipated in budget documents and related materials, such as DoD's Selected Acquisition Reports. Thus, the figures in this report for individual programs should not be interpreted as independent cost estimates for those programs; such analysis is beyond the scope of this report. Programs that may be particularly susceptible to additional cost growth are noted in the sections of this report that describe the uncertainty in CBO's estimates. To quantify additional costs for research, development, and procurement for nuclear forces as a whole, CBO estimated cost growth on the basis of its analysis of historical cost growth in analogous programs.[35] Given that approach, CBO's estimates for individual portions of the nuclear enterprise represent expected costs if acquisition programs proceed as described in DoD's and DOE's budget documents, and CBO's estimates for the overall cost of nuclear forces represent the expected costs if the portfolio of programs in the nuclear enterprise experience cost growth similar to historical averages.

How CBO's Approach Compares With Other Approaches

The bottom-up approach that CBO used to estimate nuclear costs differs from that of most publicly available analyses, particularly for DoD's portion of the costs. Because the budget details that are readily available to the public are limited, most studies employ a top-down approach to analyze nuclear costs. A top-down approach uses the category of Major Force Program 1 (MFP 1: Strategic Forces) in DoD's budget taxonomy as the primary proxy for the department's nuclear forces and scales other elements within DoD's budget to estimate the costs of communications and other DoD-wide supporting activities based on the ratio of MFP 1 to other operational force categories.[36] CBO's approach of identifying and counting only those DoD costs associated with the nuclear mission yields an estimate of the direct costs of fielding nuclear forces, whereas estimates generated with the scaling approach are intended to reflect a more comprehensive cost of fielding nuclear forces that combines the direct costs of the nuclear enterprise with a prorated share of DoD-wide overhead and support costs.

The two approaches to estimating nuclear costs differ in several important ways. MFP 1 includes several programs (the B-1 bomber, for instance) that do not have a nuclear mission. It also includes a number of programs (such as the B-52H bomber) for which the nuclear mission represents only a portion of their activities. In contrast, MFP 1 does not include many costs that CBO categorized as nuclear, including some costs related to tactical nuclear forces, the early-warning system of satellites and radars, and research and development related to some replacement systems for nuclear forces.[37] MFP 1 also does not include missile defense.

---

33. Some cost projections, particularly for research and development and procurement, draw on analysis supporting CBO's report on the 2014 Future Years Defense Program. See Congressional Budget Office, *Long-Term Implications of the 2014 Future Years Defense Program* (November 2013), www.cbo.gov/publication/44683.

34. Ibid., Chapter 2.

35. Ibid., Chapter 3.

36. Since the 1960s, DoD's budget has been grouped into Major Force Program categories (there are now 11), which include strategic forces, general purpose forces, and research and development. Historical and projected future budgets broken out by Major Force Program are published annually by DoD in a document referred to as the "Green Book." For the most recent version, see Office of the Under Secretary of Defense (Comptroller), *National Defense Budget Estimates for FY 2014* (May 2013), pp. 110-113, http://go.usa.gov/ZatJ (PDF, 3.7 MB).

37. Most studies that rely on MFP 1 apply a scaling factor to account for DoD-wide support costs and other costs not captured in that category.

Those different approaches result in different cost estimates: In 2014, DoD's budget calls for $10.8 billion for MFP 1, whereas CBO's estimate for DoD's portion of the cost of nuclear forces in that year is $14.9 billion.

Uncertainty in CBO's Estimates

There are two primary aspects to the uncertainty in CBO's estimates of nuclear costs: The costs to execute the Administration's current plans might be more or less than CBO expects, and the plans could change. Each of those aspects has several factors that contribute to uncertainty.

Changes in Costs of Current Plans. The largest uncertainty in estimating the cost of the Administration's current plans comes from estimating cost growth. Cost growth within programs that arises because of technical difficulties would lead to higher-than-planned budgets over the 10-year period, if current plans and schedules are not adjusted. CBO's estimates are based on the most recent detailed budget documentation available from DoD and DOE, and cost estimates for individual programs and activities within the nuclear enterprise incorporate the assumption that those plans will be executed successfully and on budget. However, both departments have historically experienced substantial cost growth in some programs. For example, in a March 2012 review of 96 major DoD acquisition programs, the Government Accountability Office found that, taken together, those programs had experienced about 5 percent cost growth over the preceding year, and about 40 percent cost growth overall, relative to the first full cost estimate that DoD produced for each program.[38] Similarly, a GAO review from March 2007 found that cost growth for eight DOE construction projects ranged from 2 percent to more than 200 percent; using GAO's data, CBO found that the total combined growth in those programs was about 100 percent.[39] CBO's estimates of the total cost of nuclear forces reflect the assumption that potential cost growth will be similar to the average growth experienced by analogous historical programs. However, actual cost growth could be higher or lower.

When comparing CBO's estimates with other published estimates, it is also important to consider the uncertainty about which programs and activities should be attributed to the nuclear mission. CBO's approach involved a series of decisions about which programs contribute to the nuclear mission and, in the case of programs with both nuclear and nonnuclear missions, what fraction of costs is related to the nuclear mission. Some cases required judgment calls based on limited data, particularly in determining the relative fractions of nuclear and nonnuclear costs for systems that had both types of missions; different judgments would lead to different cost estimates.

Changes in Plans. The Administration's plans could also shift in coming years. CBO's estimates are based on DoD's and DOE's plans presented in the fiscal year 2014 budget submission and supporting documents. However, some elements of those plans are still being formulated. Changes to those plans—which could arise for various reasons—could alter the costs of executing them. For example, strategic policy about the size and makeup of nuclear forces could change. A reduction in the size of nuclear forces would probably result in lower costs; but unless the reduction completely eliminated some portion of those forces (one leg of the triad, for example), the resulting decrease in costs would probably be substantially less than the proportional cut to the size of the forces, because of fixed development and support costs and other constraints. Alternatively, a program that experienced technical difficulties (and associated cost growth) could be restructured; such restructuring often results in delays, reductions in capabilities, and decreases in quantities purchased, which affect costs.

A second factor that might lead to changes in the nuclear plans is pressure on the overall budgets for the departments of Defense and Energy that could lead to reductions in the scope of programs or to delays in program schedules. Delays could push some costs outside the 10-year period that CBO considered, which would reduce costs in the short run but might increase them in the long run (unless those delays were accompanied by reductions in the size of nuclear forces).

38. Government Accountability Office, *Defense Acquisitions: Assessments of Selected Weapon Programs*, GAO-12-400SP (March 2012), pp. 6–7, www.gao.gov/products/GAO-12-400SP.

39. Government Accountability Office, *Department of Energy: Major Construction Projects Need a Consistent Approach for Assessing Technology Readiness to Help Avoid Cost Increases and Delays*, GAO-07-336 (March 2007), www.gao.gov/products/GAO-07-336.

About This Document

This Congressional Budget Office (CBO) report was prepared as required by the National Defense Authorization Act for Fiscal Year 2013 (Public Law 112-239). In keeping with CBO's mandate to provide objective, impartial analysis, the report makes no recommendations.

Michael Bennett of CBO's National Security Division prepared the report with guidance from David E. Mosher and Matthew S. Goldberg. Raymond Hall of the Budget Analysis Division contributed to the analysis with guidance from Sarah Jennings. Justin Falk of CBO provided helpful comments on the report, as did Russell Rumbaugh of the Henry L. Stimson Center and Linton Brooks, former Administrator of the National Nuclear Security Administration. (The assistance of external reviewers implies no responsibility for the final product, which rests solely with CBO.) Eric Labs fact-checked the manuscript.

Christine Bogusz edited the report, Jeanine Rees prepared it for publication, and Maureen Costantino designed the cover. An electronic version is available on CBO's website (www.cbo.gov/publication/44968).

Douglas W. Elmendorf

Douglas W. Elmendorf
Director

December 2013